Fifteeners

By the same author

POETRY
Nervous Arcs
Botany Bay Document
The Hanging of Jean Lee
My Secret Life (chapbook)
The Fall
Vertigo: a cantata
the sonnet according to 'm'
the Book of Ethel
kindness (artist's book)
XIII Poems
Jack & Mollie (& Her)
Euclid's dog: 100 algorithmic poems
Warlines
The Cyprus Poems (chapbook)
element: the atomic weight & radius of love

CHILDREN'S POETRY
Sukie's Suitcase
Barkwoofggrrr!

EDITOR
The Weekly Poem: 52 exercises in closed & open forms
Prayers of a Secular World (with Kevin Brophy)

Fifteeners

Jordie Albiston

PUNCHER & WATTMANN

First published in 2021
Published by Puncher and Wattmann
PO Box 279
Waratah NSW 2298

http://www.puncherandwattmann.com
puncherandwattmann@bigpond.com

A catalogue record for this
book is available from the
National Library of Australia

ISBN   978-1-922571-00-7

Design by Andy Szikla

Printed by Lightning Source International

This project has been assisted by the Australian Government
through the Australia Council, its arts funding and advisory body.

Speech is the small change of silence.

—George Meredith

Contents

{ The Cloud of Unknowing }

The Cloud of Unknowing

§

however this Poem has come to your
possession   whether you have bought borrowed
or been warded it   you should neither read
it nor hear it nor speak it aloud un-
less you have   by true will & by an whole

intent   purposed yourself as a ready
pursuer of the Poem   not only
in active reading but in absolute
point of ruminative reading   the which
is possible by *time* in this present

life of a living mind yet abiding
in this deadly body   for else it is
not for you   if you shall read hear or speak
it aloud   I charge you to take the time
to read hear & speak it aloud again

§

fleshly janglers   open praisers   blamers
of others   tellers of trifles   ronners
& tattlers of tales & all manner of
judgers   care I never that they ever
saw this Poem   for mine intent was not

to write such a thing unto them   & I
would that they not meddle therewith   neither
they nor any of these curious or
lettered or unlearned readers   who though
good people   this Poem accordeth nothing

to them   but it be to those readers who
stir after the secret spirit of all
Poetry   its *specials* & *dooms*   & they
full gracious disposed to be called by the
Poem   to be one with Poetry   or none

§

ghostly friend in Poetry   fastened to
words by a leash of longing   what weary
wretched heart is that the which is not a-
wakened with the breath of the Poem &
the voice of its calling!   read on then &

briskly!   you are fortified & made whole
by no work so much   & yet it is the
lightest work of all   travail therein till
you feeleth its pleasure   both in physic
& psyche   though the first time you may find

but a darkness   {& this is the cloud of
unknowing}   you may not full understand
save that you feeleth a *something*   both in
body & mind   & if you busily
travail   I trust you shall enter the Poem

§

the Poem is the shortest work of all that
you may imagine   never longer nor
shorter than is an atom   the which {by
definition of philosophers in
the science of astronomy} is the

least part of time   & it is so little
that for the littleness of it   it is
indivisible & may be nearly
incomprehensible   but this is nought
to whomsoever shall dispend some term

in the reading   stalwart but mistily
& with a sharp dart of longing   for time
is neither longer nor shorter   no more
or no fewer   than exists in one hour
here on earth   as are atoms in one *now*

§

a prelude to Poetry—   all Poets
that have ever been   or ever shall be
& all the works of those same Poets should
be hid in a haze of forgetting   &
if you come to this haze   & dwell & work

therein {as I bid}   you will see the cloud
of unknowing descend on you & all
Poetry   & so position a haze
of forgetting   that you may peruse a-
new   for of all the other scribes & their

scribblings a reader may have fullhead of
knowing   but of Poetry itself   can
no reader *think*   for why?   Poetry may
be loved but never thought   by love it may
be gotten   holden   but by thought   nay so—

{ Poem on Life }

Poem on Life

—a response to Inger Christensen's 'Poem on Death'

Something is happening   each dawn I sit
Before this papery reliquary
& it happens—   I am like an ancient
Who has swallowed all sorrow & I lift
My hand & I write—   I sit here like a

Swallow that has dashed to the ground & I
Open my beak & I sing—   it feels some-
How too late   too ungrateful to think of
Life when you have never quite lived—   it means
That every time you look yourself in

The eye   you look life in the eye & you
Weep—   like a clear question to the answers
You have carefully heard & even more
Carefully unheard—   I can hear something
Beyond my own squawk   I can hear something

So layered with moments—   & stained with love
That it echoes it echoes & rings—   &
It all trickles out   inflections of life
Like *church bell   Tintagel   Altona   a
Flute*   & who knows these things but me   *grace note*

Grammalogue   gravitational waves— it
All trickles out even *poetry*   that
Peculiar note only a wretched
Few have endured—   what if we did not have
To live   what if we could always be un-

Living   here in this heaven of un-clock
& un-light   what if we could always be—
Last night I dreamed my dogs they lived & came
Running & together we were running
& alive—   last night I dreamed that I had

Children & those children had children &
We opened our beaks & we sang—   it was
A song no one heard   not even the stone
Or the boulder on which I sat—   I was
Frightened to live like that in life's bright   I

Was frightened o yes to be—   all the life
That an awkward person must go through in
The awkward course toward death—   all the life
That is missing in the eyes of the dead
Was hanging in that song—   & the song was

Holy   running like a dog unto the
Kingdom of life—   it is lonely to think
Of life in February with the frail
Southern sunshine endeavouring light—   &
In Logan Park feebling its shade beneath

Trees   those Moreton Bay Figs & their dark—   all
Kinds of living wandering the town   I
Try but don't speak how can I—   one with the
Tattoo he cannot remove or get why
Ink persists—   one with the wife   lamented

Yes dead   whom he walks about   blue hat on
Head   with Labrador & heart—   one with no
Word that finds pronouncement   the unhappy
Language that happily fails—   whose vowels trail
Whose consonants strew their own & lovely

Virus—   like a thousand thousand fishes
Flying   & they all trickle out in the
End—   the body is a thing that does what
It must it does & insists on wild joy—
You summon the sea   o here-behind shore

With no life before love   only after—
That space where the living & un-living
Meet   somehow in the great desolation—
Write of life   pick up your pen & ponder
It   *life*   in the face of life—   you are a

Mute   & the mute cannot speak but the mute
Can from time to time write—   try to scramble
A word about life   has life a meaning
What—   now that the apple is modified
Stupid   & the earth worth nothing   what is

Life— now that the fruit has no use for tree
No knowledge of the vocable it once
Announced— on the branch by the breast at the
Beautiful beach that very first word {   }—
What is life but love dashes forth & it

Crashes to ground & it sings— words live like
Swallows their tracery crooning like this
From the page— words live like apples stupid
Modified but edible still & not
Dead— they occupy us with their bloom &

Bluff— though each are born innocent enough
Adolf Altona until we forget—
How to live how to love how to sing with
Our beaks— for love is the thing yes love is
The spring from which we the living must drink

{ Fifteen Fifteeners }

book

your eyes are the open book you open
unto me   a synecdoche of larger
unread self   I thieve a look from time to
time at shelves & shelves of chronicle &
non-blue-pencilled rhyme   your eyes are volume

justified   a margin has its lash   &
loving is intensified by browsing
you like this   sentence tells its salty tale
& little words dig deep   a story is
an elementary blink   below that lid

you watching watching makes a passion grow
& big   a pupil learns its lesson best
in ink   if I could library for an age
the sweetness your eyes give   my pleasure would
be registered   & I would pleasured live

remember

remember! remember! the long day we
are dead   half a silent century of
this   we do the proper living things   our
feet proceed   our tongues comply   & no one
knows but us   on separate ships on separate

seas on broken boats & wet   we row the
years & growing thin continue with our
lot   until the instant   there! there!   a could
be distant edge   & there! there!   we see it
now   horizon's certain verge   & mountains

rise in corridors & shadow fills the
sky   & oceans crash with continents &
black assaults the eye   & everything we
ever were   soundlessly concurs   & God
speaks & light falls through worlds & worlds & worlds

time

stun the instant instantly   prevent it
hurtling headlong into next   now is a
dog   with a whip it will sit   unclutch it
from the future it will beg   crash the clock
against the sun   wrestle a million

beams   wreck it to bits in the brightly-lit
ring   bash it   break its beautiful seams   it
is a bird   it is one of those trinkets
you wind with a key   it too can learn how
to sing   curtail the cattle of the

mind   train them according to drill   take each
by the horns & murmur a psalm   hold on
to those horns till you've broken the brute &
its ghost is gone all calm   pray   cull   acquit
like this   yes kill off your days with a kiss

proem

this is abroad   this defenestrating
into the curious view   this leaving
behind the previous bracing that framed
all world for you   scramble sill   unfasten
shutter   fracture glass & glory! abrupt

beneath the perfect still   detect it like
camera   dissect   resurrect it up
into scripture   yes lend it structure but
avoid the throat   glut can kill off beauty /
truth   riot can perish the thought   set brain

to least   abstain from excess   let sky be
"mountain"   mountain "sky" as one moment melds
into next   a few able splashes of
god-ink will do   contain the shriek   restrain
the lavish   Doric the Rococo view

graffito

the poet of the brush draws memory
to view   & all that is forgotten watched
anew   eye controlling world   if only
for a day   paints shadows over shadow
& recalls away its pain   the poet

of the orchestra   eases what was said
soothes the hurt in retrospect   with counter-
point & chord   the poet of the playhouse
broadcasts with finesse   talks the talk & walks
the boards to lessen otherness   we who

claim to relish art   declare! with common
mind   to ever keep its poets in our
heart   she who has no talent but empty
lamp & pen   mimes the same words to the wall
ink-ink-oil-ink   again   again   again

step

forward! you say confident you know where
you go   & on you go with confidence
to black   the simple destination not
always danceable   & sometimes one wrong
action takes you back   o obstacle ob-

stacle it teaches a rethink   & foot
must be altered to fit pace   you watch your
inner awkward gait iambicky &
lame   & feel your vertices all out of
place   certain problems must be solved before

tonight you know   you know this & you know
the old melee   an algorithm finds
a fault   trips up the sun until it halts
& night has hijacked day   {but darkness is
just maths that's missed}   {you ballet it like this}

cabaret

universe is gentler & certainer
than world   big bangs clang far less than yes or
no   dialogue is worse than war   bullets
fashion cleaner wounds than words   sentences
last for centuries   recited in your

bones   self is hurled through garbled air   stutters
then   & scatters over home   colloquy
throttles solitude   swats with chit   batters
with chat   contention conflict fact-fact-fact
unwilling to fully conclude   utter

is average opera   delicate
lexicon ruined   dispatched by tongues with
little to say   they prattle & natter
confabulate until quiet explodes
itself into what   call it cabaret

box

it was a bijou box   you were never
meant to fit   all those limbs & gestures   all
those wounds   day is not vast   you swerve against
the glass   creatures of nerve need galaxies
to pound   Sunday was a spot   Monday but

a grain   Tuesday was great magnitude &
brown bear & brontosaur roamed your gaping
brain   everything is shut today   space the
penalty   you chant a mantra in your
head & package up each death & birth &

pack up all the ends   yes one day may be
carton   next may be crate   but learn the art
of counterfeit   take yourself to task   teach
yourself to fold & fold   another day
may find you fitting neater into it

room

this room is brain   devices whirr in a
chiastic arrangement   refrain   chorus
chorus   refrain   carolling intimate
concert with me   o such melodious
gadgetry   this room is house   it's solid

enough for ephemera   holding firm
with a granite grasp   the walls wear gloves   the
furniture hovers   the good ceiling stares
from above   this room is planet   immense
& remote   I follow myself through a

telescope   sometimes I peer at a dot
of a girl   a tininess inside a
mammothy world & the girl dreams dreams in
here   comets & atoms collect in this
room   all my darlings & dears & it booms

attic

battle in the attic!   a harrow had
at home   all the little things in line for
fight   dust versus dustlessness between the
static air   everywhere about to burst
despite   look your sights are narrowing   they

won't or they will   hit the tidy target
in the heart   spell it out   "world"   it troubles
on the tongue   & one by one your startled
calms depart   you stand divided   self to
self   o these mortal brawls!   knowing how the

rules are rigged   & he who wins takes all   one
of you endeavours   the other never
even tries   one of you will rise again
to breathe ungodly life   the other falls
in prompt farewell   contented with the prize

tenant

it enters you   sudden   then inhabits
won't get out   settles back & laughs you are
a house!   its fastness is a teaser to
make you think it slow   you ask was that just
now or centuries ago   it is your

gorgeous accident   your who can ever
tell   & in your head   again! again!   that
un-muted bell   the time has come you need
repose   you shut up one by one   & if
you are a house! then you are closed   the hours

mimic dutiful   the morning has no
door   & where a window opened well it
isn't anymore   the moment is once
vacant & blossom everywhere   then you
wilt   tenanted   & spring was never there

puzzle

I ordered my soul today   began by
sorting   sense   shade   shape   size   located the
pieces with one flat side   & placed them on
a tray   border was fast & so was sky
one cloud led to another till the sun

up & died   next   trees   not so easy   too
many tangles   too many leaves   but some-
how things progressed   the grass was hardest   an
army of memory   every blade flashing
a further offensive of green   but bit

by bit   an odd little house on its odd
little hill   with a difficult door &
an even more difficult grille   in fact
I confess almost tossing the lot but
did not   nay!   I ordered my soul today

water

the sky zipped up like a black body bag
or a cold case finally closed   we held
our breath & stuck out our tongue it was rain
that interested us most   & we heard
California had run out of water

but the Seychelles were drowning two by two
& some were fleeing tsunami & tide
while others yearned flooding & sought it   our
suburb was piped & plugged quite superbly
we rationed our wet with finesse   we watched

one home get covered with sand another
with mud nowhere near us   our nation was
favoured when all of you lost so much more
than a house   how we wish we could say   just
for today   may you rest your world in ours

break

a spirit into splinters   or a night
into day   the quavers levitating
just the same   see a kind of orangeness
tinge the wrenched event   & head falls & sun
caws & moon forgets her name   a muteness

is the music played for spills of vital
force   taciturn the violin   still the
metronome   the birds are always first to
know   a murmuration leaves   then the dogs
who sniff the wind & go   & when you wake

to world again you have no industry
but this—   wretchedness conducting nerve to
ground   & it bothers you & bothers you
as though it were a thorn   another dawn
upon December   broken & profound

poetry

dear birds   populate my page but resist
descent   take wing   hang happy the spill &
decorate space   your fastidious flight
my equivalent   dear birds   extend your
everyday feathery   arrive in a

covey or one at a time   feel free   climb
the steep cloud & put straight thought   collocate
codify   classify   claim   you save the
whole slender mind   dear birds   I value your
random blowing my way   your patterns of

passionate state   you have my ovation
for order & form & for all the blanks
of late   dear birds   forget tree & leaf   you
are sky   let the old universe waver
& die   let gravity savour her grief

{ Remedy for Eternal Unrest }

Remedy for Eternal Unrest

We lay ourself down unto the bed as
If to sleep as if we know how to sleep
We take our hand & place it here just let
It rest caress the sheet the 100
Percent Egyptian sheet forget forget

The surreal unrest in the Middle East
& everything else but quality sheer
& beneath the sheet & beneath the sheet
We perceive through the threadcount a sheepskin
Protector to protect us from all the

Named & nameless to keep us dreaming &
Beneath the sheepskin yes underneath a
Mattress costly fit for a queen it is
Made from latex & weighs a piano
The men could barely lug it up the stairs

—

& beneath the bed yes deep down below
A Berber rot woven by poverty
But machined in a non-sub-Saharan
Factory only for us & with Love
& we sense that love coming up through the

Bed the sheepskin protector & peaceful
Sheet right into the palm of our hand &
Above the bed yes over the bed with
Our body prostrate & our palm-down hand
A ceiling that prohibits the named &

The nameless those too-huge things we just don't
Understand & we do not dream gun &
We do not dream nation & our hand is
Aware of pleasant sensations in a
Safe situation deep inside this place

—

& outside this place where our hand rests palm-
Down on a peaceful bed between ceiling
& floor yes beyond this place of windows
& doors & pictures on walls a more wide
Place of people & streets that despite the

Odd hoon & fuck-you-all screech is likewise
At peace & the shops are all open &
Trains trundle past & there are birds in the
Trees & trees in the park & the lake &
The river sparkle & swell & the sea

Yes the sea is out there as well & we
Perceive all the ships & we do not sense
War & the finest white sand inhabits
The shore cleaned fresh as the fresh cleaned sheet on
The bed where we presently rest our hand

—

& further away how much further from
Here a vaster version a much larger
World a world we don't know a world where such
Dreamers as we never go where half of
A headline can bury a being & mass

& megalopolis are too hard to
Say the place the place where under the bed
Children take cover & protectors are
Masked & sheets are of metal & windows
& walls are quite empty of air & the

Streets screech with more than the sound of a tyre
& the shops are all shut & the oceans
All oily & the land in the foreground
Lies calmly palm-down & that hand we can
See has been blown from the arm of a child

—

& that is the world of the named & the
Nameless the world of those things we forget
& forget & how can we reckon in
Our dreamy head the witless with wisdom
The nothings with nil & the leaders with

Leading the quick from the dead & these are
The questions we try not to ask as we
Tenderly lower our hand onto bed
Allow it gently to rest here palm-down
& we say to ourself this-is-our-life

The finest of quality anyone
Can buy & we feel the clean freshness &
Feel the protection yes *this is the life*
& we murmur it dreamily good-night
Good-night & lie down to sleep in it tight

{ Omegabet }

Apple

In the end man uncreated that which
God had so carefully made   & the earth
Was without form again just as it was
Before the first day   & darkness covered
The face of the deep & there was no light

At all   & the firmament sagged beneath
Gulag & slag & everyone gagged on
Aerosol   & the waters began to
Warm & rise & the grasses & green things
Modified   & the fish & the fowl &

The beasts of the land went unblessed & un-
Able to multiply   & just as the
Apple plummets below   you know man has
Rent his earthly dominion & rendered
It dead   & lo   it is dreadfully so

Bee

Varroa destructor traverses the
Tasman to permeate Australian
Territory   2030   & these
Are the world's only honey bees free of
The mighty varroosis disease   a hop

Skip & jump over the ditch & the mite
Alights   & one by one the brood-cells are
Entered   bombs are laid   & the host leaves its
Hive commandeered   the 8-legged coin-
Shaped vampiric foe works far harder for

Less than your standard bee   & one by one
The communes collapse & the queens & their
Fans are vanished to black & by springtime
None can be seen   except for her   alone
With her sting   wobbling around on {   } wings

Chance

Our last shot at love   love's loveliest tongue
Still purring on manual   not quite yet gone
Automatic   it is Yuletide today
& no one around   just a toe in the
Sea   a recalcitrant poem   & you

With your heart down below   happy xmas
To all & a merry new year   we wish
To see one again   despite the past &
Covids to come   we place all our hopeness
In this our small love   with its smatters &

Smiles   how it levels the static!   we are
Born with a bit though it feels like an in-
Finitude   we cross all our fingers &
Dot all our futures for love for love to
Endure-endure   as swiftly it eludes

Daughter

Tomorrow's forecast 95 percent
Chance of fear   animals animals locked
Inside you   a slight probability
Of tears   she texts you & says how the years
Are short but the days are long & you know

What she means what she does not mean & you
Hasten to answer today is a sun
Though you know all the clouds each by name   &
Then she arrives & her face is a star
Lit like a flower in your boring black

& you don't want to crush this delicate
Ray & you don't want to step on the cracks—
For she is the one who undarkens the
Night & she is the one who delivers
The light back into what's left of a day

Elephant

The matriarch stands in the ivoried
Graveyard   knowing she is the last of her
Line   she lowers her bones into those of
Her kin   & the age of the elephant
Dies   savannah-savannah   her great hulk

Of memoir has lumbered & lumbered for
Seventy years   evading both cirque &
Jacklight's terrain   & all days & nights are
Held in her fathomless brain   she sounds her
Going in tones I can't hear   sways famous

Fifth limb & sailcloth ears   & this summit
Of puckers   this mosque of tusk   this final
Freight of largesse & love declines unto
Dust   & the tiniest grasses pitch &
Sigh   & the sun switches off with her eyes

Frontier

The primal frontier is conceived in a
Dream   pre-landscape pre-language pre-life   an
Eager one spies his staircase to heaven
& snares himself a bride   soon you are you
Though you don't know it yet   & you grow bibs

& bobs to aid your endeavour   a heart
To be fractured   a soul to dissolve   a
Brain to grasp & forget   once your hand can
Reach a thing   next day you can join things to-
Gether   then you are taught how to take what

You make & pull it thwack! asunder   &
Thus proceed the years-years-years   you produce
A grin & grind it to tears   the final
Frontier is perceived post-breath   you can just
Make out the old rusty sign it says death

Gasp

It comes from a gill   perhaps bristlemouth
Eelpout viperfish   something below the
Photic zone   but there is no one left to
Tell   every marine snowflake has thawed   the
Blind daily grind between continental

Slope & seamount has ceased   & the friendly
Blanket of winding plankton & protists
Has long since sunk   these are the days of the
Seventh waves & they come & they come &
The sea is displaced & the whole ocean

Dumps itself just like that!   beached like a whale
In despair   & our strange & slippery
Beast of the deep flips & flops in an ag-
Ony of light   {& then with a *small*   a
Softly   she drowns in a great flood of air}

Hurrah

For what?   there are banners bunting chanting
Cheers   & streamers & slogans line the street
From right up there to down here   trumpets
Trumpet & loveless letters litter the
Air like confetti   a dog has a scratch

& the crowd starts to itch with concerns both
Profound & petty   flyers & flags hang
Like baubles from gallows   & soapboxes
Shriek from corner to corner as common-
Wealth law allows   police police parties

Of people people everywhere lauding
High praise   the whole of the country the whole
Of everyone commonly joined in this
Day of days   celebrate! celebrate! now
But for what?   hip hip hooray   we forgot

Iceberg

How lovely she looks   A-68   in
Her frills & flounces & floes   as she splits
From family & Larsen Ice Shelf &
Splinters & off she goes   it is a white
Wedding as convention calls   & Father

Time arrives on time to give his daughter
Away   Wiki proclaims no predicted
Path at this point—   there is no sense of fate
At this stage   no matter   the bride is dressed
In tatted perfection   her lacework face

Astounds   & despite observations that
Forecast destruction on all domestic
& universal grounds   she sees the good
Sea & the good sea is warm   & with a
Galumph she marries & melts in his arms

Jungle

It is a tangle this muck of stuff this
Wrangle of too much self   you monkey your
Way between chaos & calm & the deep
Blue sea of self help   o where is the palm
That billows the breeze the bandolier

Of parts   & where the song of macaws in
Trees that soothes the scofflaw's bad heart   no trunks
Or leaves for what you have found no branches
To string up your vine   & you weep for the
Lot you maybe have lost & the loss of

The whole shebang   but look!   a glister there
On a wing   & listen!   glissando on
Some wild wind   & how it all tinkles just
For now   & you are you for a moment
Or two   & something inside of you rings

King

You dysplastic despot you ruler of
Ruin   you blight us from the inside   your
Fiefdom of force has never diminished
Your law over life never died   what is
It you see when you gaze from your garret

Upon your prodigious preserve   a sun
Gleaming down on shadows that glitter   a
Moon beaming brightly on shoulders all bent
At the nerve   what is it you feel when your
Vassal comes needing   her cells bleeding light-

Ly as snow   & pleading for mercy &
Asking for grace & asking why don't you
Know   dear king your protectorate appears
Distressed   {brain of brutish   heart in a mess}
Perhaps your reign is almost over   {bless—}

Letter

Seventeen writing-tool amnesties &
Cursive & block chirography under
Lockdown & global ban   to scrawl in this
Manner means self-imposed danger   even
Kids cannot jot in the sand   o the old

Thrill of penning a note   the quickly-licked
Philatelic prize   & o the pleasure
Of reading that note   like eavesdropping with
Your eyes   a girl picks up an envelope
Addressed pre-censorship law   there is no

Box at the recipient's house so she
Pokes it under the door   & thus in a
Post-postal service world   delivery
Is achieved   & a letter is held in
A person's hand   hand-written   hand-received

March

The initial fingerlings of green through
Cracks in the north—   deciduous trees &
A few falling leaves to the south—   o brave
Little barrage of days   blind believing
You all go forward toward an April

Or May   the calendar clicks on the desk-
Top the wrist   one two & three then the Ides
& then this   the last thirty-first   it is
Thursday of course   the Roman & Old Norse
Gods face off & the sky is not massive

Enough   o tempest typhoon   terror of
Twisters   o mother of all monsoons   &
The sun eclipses a morel-shaped moon
& thundery curses from Jupiter /
Thor   & then suddenly Mars is no more

Name

It comes from the sire in a moment of
Errored desire   despite the good fight the
Rule resists & praxis transfigures it
Into immutable right   the womb is
A truth but the mother a myth & though

Half the earth is populus feminum
The birth of a girl is but property
Masculum & it just becomes fact that
Is that   o mater of mine   what art thine
Divine appellation   I seem to re-

Tain an account of your name in that part
Of my being taboo   & I thumb through
The temple the ledger of life   often
Get close to a mum or a wife but some-
How seem to miss any listing for *you*

O

O dram knave blue   come bloweth thy h'rn   to
Thy minions in meadows   thy fellows in
F'rm   anon is the time to waketh from
Sleep   & sleeping 'r waking behold thy
Sweet sheep   o jolly sheph'rd   in whom we

All trusteth   thee knoweth f'r thee we wilt
Killeth & dyeth   we knoweth thy pow'r
So sayeth all men   & we gazeth &
Waiteth f'r thee amen   but whither art
Thee with thy hurlyburly scars   is't thee

Und'r yond roof with thy stripes & thy stars   shalt
We shaketh thee from thy festinate state
& disarmeth thence to liveth our days
{& those days   o dram knave   not one wasteth
Hence   but beest filled with joy & nay harmeth}

Prayer

Hey you which art everywhere-everywhere
Give us what we want & more   if we own
One home then why not another   if we
Own one nation then why not the one next
Door   yea forgive us our wrongs & what does

It matter   the things we did/didn't do
& remove our debts   the interest ex-
Cessive!   {too much work leaves too little time
For you}   deliver us from our conscious
Mind   & grant us a goodness night's snooze   lead

Us in our campaign with the devil   so
Everyone might know whose evil is
Whose   for ours is the kingdom in which we
Bask   the power the power   {& never
Forget the glory the glory don't ask}

Question

The first question hangs like an atom in
Space & inside that question babies &
Seraphs embrace   & forests & farms &
System logistics & words & works of
Art   it is a very good question &

The world replies in kind   prosperity
Prospers conquerors conquer & pop &
Folly succour & skew the mind   & should
We could we & of course why not & some-
Where something gets quite forgot   okay fast

Forward   the fugitive babies fattened
With lack   & the last question hangs like an
Atom in black   not quite like the first yet
Somehow not new with its ruin & wrack
O goodbye Australia   I loved you

Revelation

A time of great ugliness fell in flakes
Malformed & nothing like snow   we were the
Great unblessed   there was nothing anywhere
Anymore we did not own or know   how
Doomful the day when mystery   stops   &

The dream is all dreamt & the locks are all
Locked & the ten thousand times ten thousands
Of angels with singing & harps & their
Song has also just   stopped   o where the four
Horsemen   the trumpet & thunder   o where

The key to the bottomless pit   & why
These four winds all blowing the earth & blow-
Ing the earth all to bits   whoops it costs too
Much   this *carefully*   how I yearn for the
Time when the day opened wide & for free

Supper

A table of measures & out of date
Graphs   a cloth of the finest white ash   hub-
Caps for plates & fingers for forks & we
Know it is not coming back   but we know
How to hunger & how to say grace though

God is gone awol & can't hear our thanks
For the absence of mountains for mountains
Of disrupt & waste   o yes there is food
& before the befores & after the
Afters the offer of stuff we ingest

Just like laughter   meanwhile a lightshow
Of colour & shape hitherto unknown
Unto humans   & we know & we know
It is not coming back   this world our world
& we sit ourself down & consume it

Tuesday

All days have a shape   Tuesday was always
Prickly & sharp   with hourly blades & barbs
Sticking out   Tuesday & I were not in
Good shape as I cautiously lived through my
Doubts   until you arrived   August twenty

Nineteen-eighty-five   those ovoid eyes &
Their fathomless stare & at the end of
Each arm the tiniest star clutching un-
Clutching the air   curve replaced corner &
Arc resolved edge as new geometries

Came into play   my heart & my head no
Longer more bent than the day   with a smile
Things aligned & a yawn settled time as
Your little soul redrew the world in the
Round   Tuesdays yea all days are circles now

Upon

The sweet frozen soul takes its time to un-
Freeze   the factors of winter are many
& cold   an interior ice age can
Stretch into ever   endure for aeons
Unheard of   untold   it has been a good

Season already   the fact this region
Is largely unknown is proven by so
Few tracks in the snow   & this lack of chart-
Ing the reason why nobody goes   I
Am that nobody now   can point to a

Flag stuck into a core & say there! I
Have been to that pole!   & though I am more
Or less the same girl who set forth one time
To explore   my future is gone   my past
Undone   my somebody all once upon

Valentine

I believe we belong   we have made a
Place & will live here till death   I believe
When we meet & I never waver   in
Lightness or darkness   with/without breath   for
Decades I dream   describe you to X &

Next you appear from that dream   I do not
Believe I forge you alone   whittle your
Being from air or stone but believe we
Are god-bombed & two become one & o
The explosion of fractions in fusion

A thing to believe in   astonishing
Union   & here we stand both believers
In kind   living the love we were meant to
Find   & as the sun warms itself by our
Rays   we believe ourselves into the day

Waltz

One two three slips your soft Danube shoe a-
Cross the Stygian floor   you know these steps
Backwards with fingers on keys though your feet
Never danced them before   nine decades of
Bechstein echo the hall with Beethoven

Brahms & Bach   those earliest sounds in my
Head as I lay in the dark   not sleeping
But waiting   awake to your playing that
Eased my unease & drew me some place quite
Away   & now it is you   in your soft

Danube shoes   &-how-can-it-be-you   as
You silence your way over Stygian
Floor   forever the father but father
No more   & you bow & then leave   all light
On your feet   your dance card perfect   complete

X-ray

Flash! the dark become glare   the bones all bared
& the positive pared back to black   gone
Ingenious igneous process   gone
Primordial mantle & magma to
None   no longer present the physical

Lot   no longer visible due to the
Exquisite light   o what a spectacle
Spied from heaven   & o what a lesson
For us & our radiant children   flash!
The future has landed   brilliant & bright

& everything glows through this razz-dazzle
Night   what chemical active apart from
This blessing   what vegetable mineral
Message to still be allowed   {see even
Our souls are glaring & luminous now}

Yawp

First at your breast   next at your knee   the rest
Everywhere for centuries   remember
The hand on the still-glowing stove   the hand
Serrated in red by a green that seemed
As soft as a dove   how many more since

Those tiny scraps of mishap & nature's
Sword   those sweetful bruises of fright & frond
How many more   a thousand years later
I still yelp & bawl   at the break-up the
Break-down of me & it all   & you   al-

Ways you   an indefinite figure in
Apron & gloves   fixing the frame of your
Definite love   I hold up a photo
Of what I hold dear   & the background is
You & the foreground & you are right here

Zed

The last zed was uttered like most uttered
Zeds   just after antepenultimate
Ex & penultimate wy had been said
It was a Wednesday morning   the children
Were singing the ay-bee-cee song when the

Place was surrounded by hieroglyphs who
Shot all the litterae dead   they came in
Their millions over the borders filling
The vowels & consonants with dread   & tongues
That fluttered in twenty-six letters were

Driven to babble instead   we were told
To relinquish the old alphabet we
Had loved & written & read   & on a
Normal Wednesday morning   the new order
Vanished forever the ultimate zed

{ Boy }

Boy

Boy is arrived   his boat almost broken
but still afloat   his wings still sticky from
tricking the mirrors   his insider self
turned out like a loaf of warm bread   see how
he sees us move about   watch as he pulls

the night from under our feet   Boy is a
beacon   he sparkles in darkness & kills
off black   he blinks on/off as tall ships pass
by his light   when he sleeps our eyes fill with
ocean   we call out his name   we spell out

his home   we tell him to always come back
to us   we tell him to return   & Boy
is a bell! & Boy is a bell!   he wears
his bones all fresh from the foundry & peals
between the air   world is huge but Boy is

tiny   we lose him & find him from breath
to breath & o we have stuck him so fast
to breast & he is perfect entire   who
can possess this prince of first mornings   who
can hinder his very & vast   yes Boy

is too much for our never & not of
a heart   we want him locked in our pocket
forever   we want him in garden   "tree"
"rock"   "petal"   "leaf"   his face turned to sky   his
face turns to "sky"   & Boy touches cloud   &

Boy catches sun in his fist like this   &
Boy catches us   off guard   once we are nought
& living is little & less   but Boy
is a treasure   we measure ourself by
the beauty of Boy & pray to his hands

& fingers & wrists   & pray to his toes
& feet   we witness the flam behind soft
fontanel   {ossification not yet
complete}   we witness the delicate fall
of a lash   {incarnation not fully

achieved}   one foot with angel   one foot with
world   he hovers the possible   Boy is
future   he makes things certain & centre
& just   he makes our yesterday known un-
to us   he makes tomorrow anew   &

"day"   "night"   we see how he eases the hours
to years   we see how he brings us the pear
the papaya the peach in his mouth &
Boy is delightful! & Boy is nourish
enough   once we promulgate war! war!   &

"wrath"   & "wrest"   & "ration"   & "run"   & Boy
is not with us then   & we know no joy
& our hand is a gun   this is before
Boy is come   before Boy arrives we love
{not}   we multiply {not}   we divide &

divide & divide   hear us as we are
taken away   hear us made prone   hear us
broken in low defeat   & o we are
beaten until Boy is come   & Boy is
a sum! & Boy is a sum!   he trades the

nearly & not quite with quite   he adds us
remarkably up   see how he sees us
crash & collide   & "end"   & "finish"   &
"near"   & "nigh"   Boy is so dear   we spend him
with thrift & cautiously   we save him for

after & when   once we are homeless &
no kingdom claims us & no country owns
us & we are stumbling then   o feel the
earth & the heavens full rumble   & "flood"
& "fire"   & this word "famine"   & this word

"feud"   this is many times many before
"plenitude"   this is before—   Boy is a
teacher!   & Boy is a clock!   he wakes in
the east where the birdsong is best   & sleeps
in the west with the birds   we set our watch

by his tremulous cry & bring him the
evening & daytime to bless   & Boy brings
us lesson & testament   & Boy brings
us to him   we confess unto Boy for
what we have done & what we have left un-

done   the waste the slur the ungentle word
on a gentle tongue   & we are rueful
& o tomorrow shall bring less harrow
& o we shall bring only happy to
him   & Boy is a window!   & Boy is

a rose!   opening-opening unto
the stem of "moment"   "instant"   "exigent"
"now"   he unshuts our ear & uncloses
our eye until we are all opening
too   & the spaces between dissolve &

retreat   & the separate sovereigns meet
& embrace   & the armies sign treaties
& date them Time of Boy   & in the arms
of the new universe we turn our face
to the steepest blue   to the planets &

moons   & Boy is a comet!   Boy is a
star!   a celestial shower of "ice"
& "dust"   raining down upon "desert" &
"plain"   raining down upon "sea" & "lagoon"
& raining down upon us   once our song

is in minor key   we sing in minus
& negative   & we-can-not-love-we-
can-not-love   & we have no notion of
ever & next   & everything lowers
its head in time before Boy   o how do

we do before Boy   how do we know to
get up & walk   how does our tongue know to
talk   this is the baffle proffered to us
in our ailing year   in our year of rust
in our always year of dying & al-

most & this is the dark age of us   say!
say! "green" "sweet" "bear" "borne"   words unheard/ignored
by us   no issue of thought   no issue
to house   & thus we go forth   wringing our
fortune & swinging our empty in front

of our face like a flag   how we sicken
within without Boy   but world turns   & "here"
& "there"   a flicker of something we thought
extinct   & despite our dearth   *world turns*   &
despite our certain unworthiness &

despite ourself we turn with the turning
of world   & o how we know we have longed
for this   & this word "praise"   & this word "praise"
& today we begin   magnificat!
& today we begin   magnificat!

on this day of days   the brightness appears
& the dark departs & the blindness lifts
& the mountains part   & Boy is arrived
at last   at last there is light & he shines
& he shines   & Boy is a beacon!   he

sparkles in darkness & kills off black   he
blinks on/off as the tall ships pass   when he
sleeps our eyes fill with ocean   we call out
his name   we spell out his home   we tell him
to always come back to us   & he does!

he does!   Boy always returns   like the dove
to the ark   like love to the heart   like the
life we thought we would never regain   &
all through the day we hold Boy to us   &
all through the night we let Boy go again

{ The Five Wits }

But my five wits, nor my five senses can
Diswade one foolish heart from serving thee
—Shakespeare

Reason

I have no other but a woman's reason:
I thinke him so, because I thinke him so
        —Shakespeare 'Two Gentlemen of Verona'

i

Aristotle's *sensus communis* has
no place in love   Chaucer's *resoun* where things
such as love correspond to classes to
which they belong is also wrong   how then
can love be defined   my woman's pretext

informs me love is not fixed   that love is
a beast that ogles its bars   or back in
the wild transfixes existence without
any recourse to space or time   but what
do I know of all this   I am but a

woman with a woman's heart & my love
is not of this world   when my selves collapse
& divine unto him   the earth where
is it?   & clock what is that?   & reason
falls like leaves liberating from season

ii

he is you & you are me & this does
not equal reason   I see him there in
his summer supreme   perfectly powered
to activate mine & deliver my
frost unto freedom   he is you & he

is my sun   temperate & good & not
freezing   he cradles my being in the crook
of his arm   & carefuls my verglas &
all that I am against the cold & its
treason   he is you & that is enough

I have wandered the world for him   it has
taken great injures in order to lose
winter's old chagrin   yea he is you for
I think him so   I pledge my oath to him
& thee   I have always desired it so

iii

reason?   what reason!   convene reason here
I have something to say   & being queen of
my hub's dominion I hold control &
sway   reason attend!   what can you offer
before life jingles its bell   can your *do*

this   don't do that   ever compare to my
passion's compatriot call   dear reason
do not underestimate my little
companion love   do your addition &
your subtraction   calculate low from a-

bove   reason?   what reason!   you are but fraud
thinking to outwit feeling   indeed your
glory has no heart & you are all out
of beating   he is love & I think him
so   & so goes the end of this story

Instinct

Beware instinct—the lion will not touch the true prince:
Instinct is a great matter
        —Shakespeare 'Henry V'

i

instinct lugs you by the nose   saying *touch*
don't touch   go   don't go   you can never know
the astonishing things she knows!   how she
maps the moment of each bit of day   how
she marshals the minutes by hunch alone

& tugs you on your way   this inward wit
machines folly too   incantations &
potions & false garden paths that promise
diversion from the bitterer parts life
offers daily to you   you follow your

gut to the massif top or is it the
great below   & that vista before you!
a *yes* or *no*   o how she is fickle
this faithless friend   who tells you the world is
only beginning   never at its end

ii

you want to feel you don't want to feel the
thornier moments today   instinct puts
the cup in your hand   you sip the philter
but find it a poison concocted to
squeeze the sun right out of the day   & the

more you chug the more instinct cheers   praising
stupor & how it distracts   & you strive
to stare her in the eye   but the draft has
rendered things black   you watch it pluck the light
from your view & place you in a swoon   &

you ferret for instinct everywhere
but she has long left the room   yea instinct
is good for nothing other than making
you less than a man   but then who cares!   &
bottoms up!   {you salute yourself again}

iii

you can't drive a spacecraft by instinct a-
lone   too many obstacles there in the
dark   it takes an unheavenly sense of
direction in order to steer a heart-
shuttle-rocket-ship back   you can't pilot

love with no chart   {see Mercator's atlas
contoured with wisdom   Peter's projection
plotted with art}   you can't indicate with
a busted blinker   your intention to
turn   your intention to change   your desire

to pause   edge it out   there is no relief
detailed for this   & so you are left a-
lone   your celestial body failing
sixth senses   flailing away in its near-
death throes   & anyway which way is home

Imagination

The lunatic, the lover and the poet
Are of imagination all compact
　　　　　——Shakespeare 'A Midsummer Night's Dream'

i

where are you my love　　on the bus yet to
come the one I just missed　　are you over
the ocean or in the empyrean
watching down on the world & me　　I have
scrutinised corners & cracks for you since

my announcement at birth　　I have sought your
face in systems & codes at apogee
& here on earth　　always your name on my
tongue unpronounceable　　always your face
unseen in my eye　　always your touch on

my flesh indiscernible　　always your
you distinct from my *I*　　o where are you
love　　above or below　　& when will this
odyssey end　　for I grow weary &
lose all heart　　& I grow weary again

ii

I allow Chaucer's *ymaginacioun*
{the most basic internal faculty
of impression} to rule my eternal
part　　I imagine a spaceship to take
me away　　I imagine a world where

my love rests here in my arms   I allow
Aristotle to rate *anima* as
not distinct from her external house   {my
body which walks me around the hours
walks my soul also of course}   I allow

Augustine to dream Alexandria
when he has never been   & although love
was there when time was invented   I must
utilise all my powers/perceptions
just to imagine my love with me now

iii

& you arrive!   I have envisaged you
in your conjured beauty & you are true
& alive   I have summoned you into
my constellation & you are a star
& thus you are stellar contrived   the gods

have listened & pitied me   & sent your
Venutian craft   & there you hover   my
unworldly lover   & there you offer
your self my exquisite draft   how is it
we have continued like this   & how have

we remained   life-life-life-life   alone &
unsustained   none of it matters any-
more   the moments or the years   no none of
it matters   for you & I have assumed
ourselves & our love & we are right here

Fantasy

It is to be all made of fantasie,
All made of passion and all made of wishes
        —Shakespeare 'As You Like It'

i

I pursue you with an inner gaze &
persuade you into external vision
with my *phantasticke* eye   this is the view
that brings you existence   this is the view
that brightly hallucinates you   I lie

in my reverie floating through night with
comets all blooming above   watching the
stars open & close   those florets of fine
cosmic stuff   I dream my dream in mirrors
& smoke that veil the debris of space &

time   I elucidate you against such
shadows within the shroud of my mind   yea
tonight is flowing with ardour & art
& I have but one wish   the trick of your
love   & tonight that is magic enough

ii

what is chimera   what is illusion
when the wild darks rise   where is the fancy
camera obscura   when it is you
before my eyes   what is *wisshen* but a
widened version of what the narrow soul

sees   & what is *apparicion* but a
being revealed by apparently
fantastic means   perhaps it is true I
no longer can tell reality from
sheer delusion   but what does it matter

heaven or hell when you are my dearest
confusion   o wherever adventure
my abstracting feet   over voids either
fabric or true   they heed one compass which
needles one place   & that one place is you

iii

never is the time to awake out of
sleep   now is the time to abide as love
deems   sliding through fires as sleek as silk
sheets   enduring wishes & dreams   all gone
the moment for dubious fact   {is that

what you meant   is this what you mean}   & in
its place theatre   unreliable
act   a stage where no queries like these come
between   I have felt this feeling beneath
moon & sun   delighting in day & de-

lighting in night   at no phase debating
that you are the one   that this fervour is
nothing but right   what difference to lovers
gospel or lie   {truth is always more strange
than fiction   for sweethearts like you & I}

90

Memory

How sharpe the point of this remembrance is!
　　　—Shakespeare 'The Tempest'

i

dear memory　faculty cradling all
detail　please forgive the amnesiac
heart　pardon its longer & shorter term
lapses in recalling love's factual
data　dear memory　container of

spatial & temporal code　excuse the
lack of retention　absolve the soul which
ignores the actual & spends its era
forgetting　dear memory　release your
charge from delivering image plainly

& without restraint　exonerate that
part of input retrieval which fails to
process with formal intent　for nothing
in love is worth neglecting　& all in
love is worth more than gold in conserving

ii

my iconic memory fast decays
its quickly filmed file of your face　you smile
then fade before my eyes & a spectre
interchanges in place　my echoic
memory similarly fails in

preserving your voice as perceived   those words
you say those sounds you pronounce fall silent
like autumn leaves   my haptic memory
somewhat succeeds in storing your touch in
my skin   but even that "partial report

paradigm" can never linger within
nay!   all I remember is flying through
galaxies vast & striving for truth   I
fly there still   hurtling through futures   hurtling
through pasts   endeavouring to recall you

iii

memory memory back on dear earth
grant a cosmological constant   it
is there in the photos   supernova
legacy   there in the theory of we
who still live insistent   o memory

memory do not sell out   the vital
for those who choose love   we are here in our
mask at the demonstration   we are here
at home in isolation   & we are
scared of—   memory memory do not

betray what makes you who you are   wishes
kisses   sweethearts running before the green
wave   sights & sounds throughout the years   the text
of life's bazaar   what history better than
such a list? a memoir of loving   *this*

About the Author

Her name is A   she has published B books
She was born in C & married D when
They were both only E   soon F appeared
Followed by G & those were the early
Years   then a divorce then a grad/post-grad

Course where she earned her H & finally
Started to scrawl   meanwhile little F &
G grew   wed J & K   & before she
Knew it L M & N crawled along   she
Downsized to O with her dogs P & Q

& wound her way as an R S & T
{Later a U} with stints as a V &
W   & so time went by in the
X of a Y during which she met Z
{& life at last made sense inside her head}

Acknowledgements

I am grateful to the editors of the following publications, where some of these poems first appeared:

Antipodes [USA], *Australian Book Review, Australian Poetry Anthology 2018, Australian Poetry Journal, Borderless Anthology of Feminist Poetry, Cordite, Dispatches from the Poetry Wars* [USA], *Hampden-Sydney Poetry Review* [USA], *Imagination in an Age of Crisis: Soundings from the Arts and Theology, Homings & Departures: An English-Mandarin Anthology* [Curtin Univ.], *I Protest: Poems of Dissent, Mountain Secrets Anthology, Rabbit*

An earlier version of the poem 'Boy' was shortlisted for the 2016 Josephine Ulrick Prize.

A reading of the poem 'Iceberg' appears on the *Australian Book Review* Podcast (September 2020), and another of 'Poem on Life' on the Australian Poetry 'Modern Elegy' Podcast (2021).

Sincere thanks to the Australia Council for the Arts, without whom these poems could not have been written.

Notes

The sequence 'The Cloud of Unknowing' is loosely drawn from the first six chapters of the late fourteenth-century Christian mystic treatise of the same title (anonymous: ed. Evelyn Underhill, John M. Watkins, London: 1922).

The epigraph on 'The Five Wits' title page is from Shakespeare's Sonnet 141.

www.ingramcontent.com/pod-product-compliance
Lightning Source LLC
Chambersburg PA
CBHW030851090426
42737CB00009B/1189